Laugh More, Yell Less:

A Guide to Raising Kick-Ass Kids

Stuck-at-Home Edition

Dr. Robert Zeitlin

Dr. Robert Zeitlin

Original Cover Design and Layout: Kristin Kane Ford
Stuck-at-Home Edition Cover Design: Devin Wachs
Cover Photo: Rob Hainer/Bigstock.com
Graphics: Bigstock.com, Kristin Kane Ford

ISBN: 0996292918
ISBN-13: 978-0-9962929-1-7 (Dr. Robert Zeitlin)

DEDICATION

To our kick-ass kids, Ian and Lilly.

Dr. Robert Zeitlin

CONTENTS

Preface   vi

Introduction   viii

1   Stepping Up   1

2   What Can You Do   5

3   How You Can Save the World   9

4   How I Learned to Laugh More and Yell Less   15

5   Zoom In and Zoom Out   21

6   Zig Zag   27

7   Play More and Work Less   33

8   Make More Time   37

9   Be the Good Witch   43

10   Climb Out on a Limb   49

11   Put On Your Cape   55

12   What's Next?   59

Acknowledgements   61

References   62

About the Author   63

PREFACE

Stay at home. Don't go out. Keep six feet away from other people. These are the new rules that we follow in early 2020. We've been following them for only a month but they already dominate our lives. And we don't know how long it will last.

What are you supposed to do when you are stuck at home with your kids 24/7? …with no end in sight?

> *I always said that I wanted to spend more time with*
> *my kids. I guess I should be careful what I wish for.*

– Comedian Jim Gaffigan

First of all … Congratulations on your promotion to homeschool teacher! … and homeschool principal … and nurse … and counselor. Not to mention running the cafeteria and physical education. Oh, and now you're the janitor, too?

We didn't realize how much we rely other people to help raise and educate our children. Now we do. It's all on us.

In 2015, I brought a message from the future. The first edition of this book asked you to recognize the uncertainty facing us. In such a rapidly-changing timeline, trading everything for an Ivy League education was a risky gamble.

As an alternative, I offered a guide to raise the kick-ass kids that the future was definitely going to need.

Well, folks. The future is here. In April 2015, I said that we can't predict years ahead. Now, sitting in my home for days on end in April 2020, I can safely say that we can't predict months ahead.

Every challenge also offers an opportunity. We can "survive" this moment and hope it never comes again. In my professional opinion, it is foolish to hope that everything will return to normal after the COVID-19 pandemic. It clearly won't.

So let's take advantage of this moment.

Think of all that you are learning about your kids … and about yourself … and about your partner. Use this new edition of "Laugh More, Yell Less" to dive in and transform "we have to" into "we get to."

You are never going to get a chance like this to make your mark as a parent. Use the added pressure to make your family and partnership stronger. Let's make this a turning point.

Dr. Robert Zeitlin
April 2020

INTRODUCTION

Having worked with youth (and raised my own kids) for almost 20 years, I know how hard parenting is and how little support there is for parents. It's often a thankless job and it's always your fault. Something has changed for me in the last couple years to give me more joy as a father. I've shifted into a new gear, giving me more power and control over my life. I stopped doubting myself so much and started laughing with my kids and my wife every day.

The path I travelled to gain more control and choose to laugh more may be different from yours. You have a different set of strengths and assets than me. We have our own kids and family situations. There isn't one Yellow Brick Road. As we all head off for Oz from different starting points, I have seven must-have items to pack for your trip. Mix and match, try them out, find your own path to laughing more and yelling less. On the way, discover your special powers and use them to create a family that raises kick-ass kids.

LAUGH MORE, YELL LESS: Stuck-at-Home Edition

1

STEPPING UP

At the end of the movie "Back to the Future," Doc Brown rushes Martie McFly (played by Michael J. Fox) and his teenage girlfriend into the time machine with an urgent message:

"It's your kids, Martie! Something has got to be done about your kids!"

Doc Brown was talking to parents in the 21st century and his message couldn't be more important: It is about your kids! The future is now.

The world needs you to raise kick-ass kids. Things are going to hell in a handbag and, to (mis)quote Star Wars, your kids are our only hope.

Climate change, religious extremism, homelessness. Our political system is more polarized and the gulf grows every day between the "haves" and the "have-nots." As I write these words, we are facing the most deadly pandemic in a century.

Raise your hand if you have an answer for any of these problems. Just one simple answer. Anyone?

Bueller? Bueller?

My wife Betsy is an amazing cook. I mean restaurant-level. But her cooking and baking skills aren't her greatest assets in the kitchen. Betsy believes that there is an answer out there for every problem. Her favorite line is "all the answers are in the library." Just like we all rely on Google, Betsy knows that there is a cookbook somewhere that can teach her how to make anything. Where she excels, what allows her to make incredible meals, is in her unshakable confidence.

But cookbooks and Google don't have recipes for the problems that our children will face. Searching for these answers can try our confidence. When we talk about terrorism or the achievement gap in education, the conversations always end with the downward stares, slow head nodding, and silence. We feel helpless because we don't know where to start or how to make a difference.

But don't give up hope yet. We have a secret weapon. Who am I and how can I remain optimistic? I have worked with youth for nearly 20 years in my office, in clinics, in schools, and in community development programs with my background in clinical psychology. I talk to teachers and work with professionals dedicated to training the next generation of leaders.

They all see what I see. We witness the potential in the kids we serve every day. We've seen your kids in action.

We get to witness them being kind and finding passion for work that inspires them. They work hard to achieve their goals, and don't bother with short cuts. They defuse tense situations with laughter and charisma and reveal their true character when no one is looking.

I am so humbled by your kids' willingness to accept differences. I have seen them stand up to bullies. I have been awe-struck by their morality and wisdom. It has been an honor to witness their capacity over the last 20 years. With an unpredictable future on the horizon, they have more to teach us than we have to teach them.

Facilitating a group of teens and parents to discuss sexuality and identity, I met a 13 year old young man who may be the next Martin Luther King, Jr. I'm not kidding. That is literally the thought that popped into my head when I heard him speak.

Cautiously, the group had opened up about their biases and confusion. Then, uninvited, this young man opened his mouth and spoke from his heart. He was so insightful and compassionate, wise beyond his years. He started by thanking a total stranger for sharing his fears saying, "I feel so connected to you right now."

Two minutes later, his empathy was so profound that I was ready to hand over the group for him to run. I swear I started to hear Whitney Houston singing "The Greatest Love of All" in my head:

"I believe the children are our future. Teach them well and let them lead the way."

We need more of these kids. We need a critical mass. We may not be able to solve the world's biggest problems but we are sitting on a gold mine. The solutions to our world-class problem are in the developing brains of your world-class children.

We don't have a library that can give us all the answers. Our job is to build one.

That's why I'm talking to you. Along with my sense of awe over your kids' potential, I hold this strong belief: Families are the most important linchpin to a child's success. Set them up right and watch the children flourish.

Parenting books sell "the" answer to channel your nervous energy. Push your kids like a Tiger Mom. Practice a skill for 10,000 hours. Focus on grit or resilience. Those one-size-fits-all recipes are taking advantage of your fear. This book is different: it's not about red flags.

We need to work together to grow the kick-ass kids that the world needs. I seek to inspire you to raise the kids who are going to save our planet and put things right.

But there's more. While pursuing your mission, you can make your whole family healthier, happier, and more loving. No, you don't have to shut off cable or run marathons. It's a lot easier than that. There's no immersion blender to buy. Put away that checkbook.

2

WHAT CAN YOU DO

Most parents want to know: How can I raise a happy child? How can I keep my child from suffering the way I did? How do I raise my child to mature into a good, kind man? or a strong, independent woman?

Many of you are working so hard to create a secure path for your kids. I know where you are coming from. These are scary times. We sign up for tutoring, prep classes, and the "right" schools. But you are grasping at straws when you try to pave a "safe" road to the future. We just don't know.

There's a message coming in. It's for you.

Hi. It's the future calling. I'm sorry to interrupt your day but I have an important message. You really can't imagine what I look like. I know you are smart but – trust me – you don't know me yet. I'm sorry if that freaks you out.

Take it from me: the future is going to be better and worse than you can even imagine.

That's why I'm calling with one request: please stop raising your kids as if you know me, as if you know what they need. It's not about packing for them. You don't need to protect your kids from me. Reacting out of fear doesn't get us anywhere.

You need to prepare them to take charge.

I am calling to stop you because I REALLY need your kid. I need what they bring. They play a big part. You don't know it yet. They don't know it yet. And neither of you can predict what they are meant to do.

Trying to predict that your daughter or son will be the next President or need an Ivy League education is wasting valuable time and energy. The world is changing so fast that it is impossible to speculate what your kids will need. You just don't know.

I do have a place where you can put all of that energy to good use. Your kids need a deeper level of preparation. And it's the kind of training that only you can provide. I have a special mission for you.

3

HOW YOU CAN SAVE THE WORLD

Right now, parenting feels like an impossible job. If it isn't the exhaustion of keeping everyone healthy, you have to deal with school and recess and all three meals and snacks and. and. and.

Even before you were stuck at home, you were just getting through. Most of the time you felt like you didn't know what you are doing. You went on instinct and reacted out of fear. At almost every moment, you worry that you are really screwing it up. And we all lose it sometimes.

Feeling lost and worrying all the time is normal. It's human to blow your top when you're under this much strain. Understanding that the fear and anger can overwhelm your senses, I'm going to ask you to push "pause" for a minute.

I know this is a big challenge, especially now.

To be honest, stuck at home for the first couple weeks, I don't think I took two deep breaths. I rushed from one thing to another. Just thinking about all the new challenges and restrictions was so exhausting!

This job was always more than it appeared to be. Now we have a whole new list of responsibilities.

As hard as it might be, for just a minute, I need you to take a breath and look up at the horizon. There will be a time after all of this. And we need to start thinking about what that will look like.

Here's something I need you to consider for a moment: Your child may save the world one day.

You may be raising the next Ghandi, Bill Gates, or Malala Yousafzai.

It may to be hard to get your head around this right now. But I have news for you: You're not just another parent. You're more. You are a like a sleeper agent. You have abilities that you haven't yet activated. You may have an idea what I am saying but you have not yet tapped into your true powers.

What if I told you that I am 100% certain that your child is destined to play a critical part in the future of the world? It sounds extreme but what if I'm right?

You can try to shake off the possibility that you are raising the kick-ass kids that the world needs. But you can't. If future-me somehow got a message to present-me that my son or daughter is going to affect the future direction of the world, I might not like it but I would have to pay attention.

Sure, that's a lot of responsibility. **Don't panic.** Remember, you have special abilities.

You bring a lifetime of valuable experiences to your job as a parent. You may think that all the mistakes you made are worthless but you're wrong. Everything that happened in your life made you who you are. Every success, failure, and misstep has value in this mission.

Let me assure you: your kids are watching and learning from you. They learn so much from the way you interact with them. The way you live your life each day carries enormous weight, more than what you say or even what you do with your kids. I want to help you tap into your special abilities to strengthen your family from the inside out. Here is the perfect place for you to start:

LAUGH MORE,
YELL LESS

Sounds simple, right? **Well, it is.**

In fact, you can start right now.

Put this book under your arm and go tell your kids a joke, find a funny movie on cable, or listen to a comedian with your partner. Gather the family around the TV or dinner table.

You will start to see a difference. You're all laughing and enjoying your time together. No one is yelling. Savor the moment. Take a mental picture. Now you have a taste of what more laughter can do for you, and your family. Do you want to do it more?

Here's where I can help. The trick is not finding something to laugh about. The trick is how to do it more, like all the time. I know it sounds impossible, a constantly laughing family, like some robotic Disney movie with sunny skies and no clouds. Don't worry, the problems will still be there. There will always be stuff to yell about. I promise.

Laughing more and yelling less is a long-term formula. A happier family is just the start of great things to come. This is only the starting point to raise kick-ass kids.

In any random day, you might laugh a little and yell a lot. I've met lots of parents who feel like they yell all the time. They can't even remember the last time they laughed hard.

Let's change the ratio so your family is the place where you get more laughs every day. When you have to yell, it won't feel so bad.

Does this sound like an improvement over how you feel right now? When you change your ratio of positive-to-negative emotions each day, funky things start to happen: you can concentrate more, your mind opens up, you feel more creative and free, and you become happier and healthier. Research in Positive Psychology backs me up here.

Here's how I can help you get there. This isn't about "turning your frown upside-down" or some short-term cure to change your mood.

This is bigger than that.

Hello? McFly? Knock, knock! Remember, this is about your kids.

My grandfather always used to smell the heads of newborn babies. It was a creepy kind of ritual. He would always say, "ah, that's the stuff of life." It seemed like he was being a life-force vampire.

Now I kind of know what he was getting at. I feel the same way when my kids make me laugh. I feel like it's a return on investment: I've shed tears for you, now you pay me back with laughter. Mostly it's confirmation that we did something right.

We did the work and set the stage for our family to have these incredible relationships. Using this solid footing, our two kids are going out in the world to kick some ass. They are leaders, thinkers, hard workers, and good friends.

Where did I start?

4

HOW I LEARNED TO
LAUGH MORE AND YELL LESS

You should know that this is all still pretty new to me. In fact, I have something to confess. I am a knee-jerk dad. You learn a lot about yourself when you become a parent, like how to get through a sleep-deprived work day or how to clean up puke stains on your sleeve. All that good stuff.

One thing I learned was that I couldn't control my knee-jerk anger whenever my kids spilled anything. I would freak out before I could even think about it. No matter how calm I was in the moment, my anger would still jump out. I felt horrible when I heard myself yelling at my kids. I was embarrassed. That's not the kind of dad I am.

Even though I have worked with youth and raised my own kids for over 20 years, none of that experience changed my reflex to anger. But things have changed for me the last couple years. Instead of ranting and cursing when my kids spill now, my shoulders do this weird thing.

They rise on their own as if my body is saying, "so what?" I didn't even notice the shift until I first heard myself giggle at the silliness of the scene in front of me. That is when it actually hit home. Pretty soon, random spills and surprises stopped cueing me to replay a horror slasher movie and turned into a slapstick scene from the Three Stooges with all the silly sound effects. Bonk! Dink! Crash!

I felt like a curse was lifted. I was becoming the parent that I thought I could be.
How did I make this change?

I'm going to lay out seven ways to unearth your special powers. The more I practiced these seven moves, the less I hulked out.

I remember asking my mentor for parenting advise when I was a panicked young father. He told me: "your job is to get out of the way and let your kids become who they are supposed to be." Get out of the way? Like get my own issues out of the way? I thought, "isn't there an easier way?"

If I knew then what I am learning 20 years later, Yoda-me could have said, "patience you must have, young Padawan." In the future, you will find ways to control yourself, build in a pause, and start laughing more.

No one tells you that, when you become a parent, you aren't always going to recognize yourself in the mirror.

It's confusing as hell sometimes. I can't tell you how excited I was to get past my knee-jerk reaction! It made me wonder what else was under my control.

How about you? What would you like to have more control over?

7 Ways to Start Raising Kick-Ass Kids

5

ZOOM IN AND ZOOM OUT

I was late to pick up my daughter from school. I tried to take a shortcut but landed in bumper-to-bumper traffic. Is there anything worse than being late, stuck in traffic, feeling like the worse parent in the class, and not being able to do anything to change it?

I wanted the superpower to make the other cars move out of the way. Like a Jedi Master, I would wave my hand, lift the cars into the air, and throw them aside. I tried. But it didn't happen that way.

What did I do instead? I yelled like a cranky boy and banged on my steering wheel and had myself a mini rage attack. I admit it. It was pathetic. Then I ran out of steam, got really still, and started judging all the other drivers. Soon enough, I regained the energy to bark orders at them to move.

Did they hear me? No.
Did it make a difference? No.
Did I feel better? Not really.

Put yourself in my shoes, stuck in a traffic jam, getting later by the minute, picturing your kid wondering where you are, feeling like a horrible parent. Let me ask you: how much control do you have: (a) a lot, (b) a little, or (c) none?

The answer depends on what you are trying to control. If you are talking about the traffic, your control level is pretty much at zero.

What can you control?

Like I said before, if you can choose your reaction, you gain control of the situation. Zen Buddhists have known this for centuries. But I learned it from Viktor Frankl.

Viktor Frankl was a prisoner in the concentration camps in World War II who lived to become one of the most important thinkers of the 20th century. After he was liberated at the end of World War II, he wrote a book called A Man's Search for Meaning where he described his experience in the Nazi death camps.

Frankl was put in the most impossible situations. At his lowest point, totally helpless to stop the torture, he chose to stop fighting. In that moment, he realized that the one and only thing that he could control was himself and his reaction. He retreated inside himself and resisted the Nazi invasion on his body. He wasn't going to let them own his reaction.

If you let your gut reflexes do the talking, you give up control of the situation and yourself. React in a knee-jerk way to whatever happens to you and you hand over your power. But if you can form the habit of responding instead of reacting, you can gain control over your life.

Like Viktor Frankl, I found untapped power in the gap I created between what happens to me and how I choose to respond. Harnessing this power helped me deal with spills and traffic jams. But the greatest difference in my life was the way Frankl's wisdom affected how I deal with my wife and my kids.

Of course, creating that gap is easier said than done. It's so much easier to try to control others, isn't it? It's hard work to control yourself. Making this change does take practice but turning the equation around will produce results in your life, especially parenting.

So try this.

Flip the script.

Zoom in on yourself and zoom out on your children.

Instead of trying to control your child, switch it up. Exert the control on yourself. And instead of showing a passing concern for yourself, show an active concern for your children. Be a better listener, show more compassion, be curious.

There is a mother I know who tried this strategy with her son. He flies off the handle at every little setback, even if he loses at a video game. He freaks out, throws a tantrum, and can't calm himself down.

She spent years frustrated that she couldn't control his behavior with punishment or taking things away. Nothing worked. She gave him space to finish his tantrum and get himself together. But that was just damage control. The tantrums kept coming and his coping skills weren't improving.

So she flipped the script.

She would zoom in on her son when he freaked out. But she hadn't thought about her reaction. When she did zoom in on herself, she realized that she was meeting her son's huge wave of emotion with another wave of her own. She also realized that his tantrums made her feel angry and scared and helpless.

So the next time he freaked out, she stopped herself from trying to fix it or calm him down. She zoomed out.

She told him, "I feel helpless to do anything for you right now. I feel scared by how angry you are." She made it clear that she wasn't expecting him to do anything.

After saying her piece, she didn't choose to escape for her safety or start yelling. Instead, she sat down with him for the first time. She gave him a different response. He wasn't left alone with his feelings. He saw that she stayed. She remained engaged but didn't follow the old script.

It didn't make a huge difference at first but it didn't have to. It got them unstuck. She felt empowered to keep trying and he didn't feel isolated anymore.

Zooming in on yourself and zooming out on your kids can give you a greater sense of control and can make you feel like a better parent.

You give yourself the space to be a role model for your kids. They see you being vulnerable, making the effort to help, and willing to show yourself some compassion.

YOUR MISSION:
FLIP THE SCRIPT.

P.S. Zooming in and out is the most important "muscle" to strengthen when you are stuck at home.

You can easily create a downward spiral when you focus on what is going wrong, worry too much about an uncertain future, and concentrate on what you don't have. This is one way that zooming in can mess you up. Zooming in can also reverse that spiral when you flex your character strengths ("superpowers").

What we focus on becomes our reality. Exercising your superpowers of gratitude, creativity, humor, or kindness can create an upward spiral of greater health and connection.

P.P.S. How much should you zoom in on the news? If you're like us, you probably have a different capacity (and need) for information than your partner. Betsy gets overloaded before I do. Does more information stabilize you? Then zoom in. Do you need to turn off the news? Then zoom out.

The one thing we all need is to give ourselves kindness and grace. Today you might need to binge that TV show, sleep late, work, or find a purpose that stabilizes you, even if it is cleaning that closet out. Tomorrow you might need to do the opposite.

Let yourself zoom in and zoom out. Forgive yourself when you go overboard. And when your eyes are starting to hurt from too much screen time, look out the window and focus on the farthest object you can see. Extra credit if it's a part of nature.

6

ZIG AND ZAG

My dad was a good golfer. He was a runner in college but as a father, he was not in any kind of shape to play other sports. He was a big man with gentle hands. Picture Fred Flintstone up on his twinkle toes (dink-dink-dink-dink-dink) at the bowling alley. Golfers need a mix of power and good hands. On a good day at the golf course, my dad had both.

There was a tournament that he always looked forward to at his golf club called The Derby. It matched up golfers randomly. He won it a couple times. The secret, he said, was being on the same page with your partner. When you play badly on one hole, that's the one where your partner needs to do well. And when he sucks, you pick him up. The times when he won The Derby my dad would say, "we zigged and zagged together."

My dad knew that there were better golfers out there. He didn't win many head-to-head tournaments. He would need to play his best round and all the good players would have to turn in their weakest round. But in The Derby format, he could harness the power of two players, zigging and zagging in tandem, to beat teams that had more skill on paper.

Parents need to wear a lot of different hats. Sometimes you need to be the heavy, the joker, the rule-breaker, the hugger, or the schedule-keeper. Parenting is a long race, not a sprint. If one parent is always carrying the load, it's like putting too much weight on one side of the car. You can't expect to get around the track a million times. Eventually you blow out a tire.

Raising kick-ass kids takes a team effort. And you are it. This is the team right here. No substitutes. Do some of your own ass-kicking by strengthening your partnership.

Parents who can get on the same page, zigging or zagging when they need to, will find more ways to win. We all have our strengths but we also all need a break from the role that we play, especially if you play the heavy.

Think of zigging and zagging like playing doubles in ping-pong. You need to be able to communicate with your partner or else you both end up frozen, watching balls beat you down the middle.

Kids benefit from knowing that their parents are on the same page. To quote Psychologist Dan Gottlieb, the greatest thing you can do for your kids is to wake up tomorrow morning and love your partner more than you did yesterday.

But how do you get there? One weird thing about long-term relationships is that we can react to our romantic partners like adult versions of the kids that we were. I resent what I'm not getting. Your emotions overwhelm me. I rebel. You disappoint me.

Resentment can stem from an imbalance in responsibilities, even if you didn't do it on purpose. Michael Kimmel, author of Guyland (2008), points to the difference in maternity and paternity leave as one way that two working parents can try to split up parenting and housekeeping tasks but still find themselves far from where they wanted to be. In "All In," Josh Levs (2015) takes a hard look at paternity leave and other ways that our "work-first" culture undermines families.

So what can you do? Try laying out the childcare and household responsibilities on paper together without any judgment. Ask if the current arrangement is a good balance for your partner. If not, brainstorm one small change and set a date in one week to see how it's going.

The goal is to be a closer team. Don't let the goal of 50/50 or "equality" to get in the way of seeking a better balance.

And, guys, you should know that research shows that doing more housework leads to more sex. Check social media for the hashtag **#choreplay**

YOUR MISSION: STRENGTHEN YOUR TEAM.

P.S. Social distancing in 2020: keeping six feet away and wearing a mask to keep your germs to yourself. When you are stuck at home, this is nearly impossible to do in the house. Which reminds me of…

Social distancing in 2019: staying late at work, shopping, wine with your friend, playing golf for hours or going on hunting trips. Before 2020, this is how we made space for ourselves and kept our family at a safe distance (from our moods, not germs).

Living in quarantine conditions can definitely highlight parts of our lives that we don't usually notice. For instance, how much we get on each other's nerves. Or how much we rely on little methods of escape to keep our sanity.

Zig-Zag Pro Tip:

Take this limitation as an opportunity. This is a time to take advantage of those little fight-or-flight moments when you start feeling something intense. You know that feeling. That's when we go to a comfort food or method of escape to avoid getting overwhelmed.

In that moment, try something new to interrupt the cycle. Drink a glass of water if you feel hungry. Pull out a piece of paper and write for three minutes if you feel frustrated. Reach out to a friend (who will listen) to share what's up.

Interrupt the mini-fight-or-flight cycles that run your habits. Turn social distancing inside-out.

If you can adapt the old ways that you usually make space (now that there is no space to make!), you give yourself a chance to understand yourself better and take care of yourself in a new way. By sticking around when you feel triggered to escape, you might find that you are more present with the people who love you.

LAUGH MORE, YELL LESS: Stuck-at-Home Edition

31

7

PLAY MORE AND WORK LESS

Many of us would like to spend less time working. "The Four-Hour Workweek" (2009) is a best-selling book because the idea of shortening the workweek is so enticing. In his book, author Tim Ferriss challenges us to take control of how we want to spend our most precious resource: time.

Think about the family time you put in with your partner and with your kids. There is always going to be a balance between work and play. You need to teach manners, enforce rules and consequences, and hold boundaries by saying "no" when necessary. Putting in this work creates a home and family life that you can enjoy and produces kids who can function in the world. If you don't lay this groundwork, parenting can become exhausting. And, of course, parents need to return to this work periodically as kids grow up to confront new social and academic challenges.

Now think about the parts of your family life you would like to spend more time doing. Snuggling on the weekend, chilling out, dressing up your dog, having a catch, or spontaneous dance parties in the kitchen. Do you get enough of this? As a parent, when do you drop your grown-up face for a minute?

• When do you slow down to savor a joyful moment?
• When do you get lost in a momentary calm?
• When can you step back to laugh at the insanity of it all?

One thing that can go out the window when we become parents is letting ourselves play. We spend our whole day cooking, dressing, cleaning, and driving our kids. It's easy to lose yourself in the hustle and bustle. Why do airlines tell you to put on your own oxygen mask before your kids'? Because your kids can't survive unless you can breathe.

The same is true here on the ground. Taking care of yourself is one of the most important things you can do for your kids and your family. For one, you will live longer. Mostly, you are being a role model for your kids. You are showing them how to live their lives in future work settings, their relationships, and one day, in parenting your grandkids.

And then we started to believe the lie that play is something that only children do. Does even loosening up a little make you feel uncomfortable? Here's a test: stand up and spin around two times. Try dancing in the kitchen. Next time, do it in front of someone else.

If we let ourselves have fun, we feel like we are slacking off or being lazy. Believe it or not, play can lead to some surprisingly intense performances. The most amazing feats of extreme athletes and inventors happened because people dove headfirst into their passion, lost a sense of time, and settled into a period of intense focus. The name for this state is "flow," also known in sports as "the zone."

In flow, you are fully engaged in what you are doing, emotionally and physically. Think of the moment that a comedian wins over an audience or a basketball player takes a last-second shot. Do it without an audience:

1. let yourself get totally immersed in something you enjoy doing.

2. savor the moment, find the beauty around you or the silence, or the perfect angle of sunlight through the window.

3. create something, even if it's just drawing with crayons or building with LEGOs, without a model or plan in mind.

4. pick out a moment in time and take a picture in your mind. Notice everything about it, remembering the tone of people's voices, focusing on the details of the setting,.

In "Authentic Happiness," Martin Seligman (2002) pointed out that we can "rush through our days without taking time out to savor the things we enjoy." He added that telling someone else how much you valued a moment is another way of savoring, and so is bragging and letting yourself feel pride.

What if you made a concerted effort to do something that

- you love so much that you lose track of time?
- you enjoy doing so much that you don't want it to end?
- makes you care less about what other people think of you?
- really serves no purpose except that you enjoy doing it?

What's your thing? Would it be dancing, hiking, singing, building models, or exercising? What can stop time for you?

Enjoy the silly moments and let yourself play. The work will still get done. In fact, it may get easier because you will have more energy. Adding more play into your day, on your own or with your family, will help you connect with each other. Getting to a moment of flow is rare but working to get there can have a lot of value, too.

If you get in the swing of seeking flow and savoring moments in your life, you will spend more time doing things you enjoy. Play more. Then working at "doing family" won't be as challenging or exhausting.

YOUR MISSION:
PUT ON YOUR OXYGEN MASK FIRST.

8

MAKE MORE TIME

I loved watching the TV show "Bewitched" when I was growing up. It was always on. Sure, I was a little in love with Elizabeth Montgomery. I'll admit it. She was hot. It didn't help that the guy who played her husband kept changing. In my dreams I could be the next Darren.

Plus, she could do magic. Just by wiggling her nose. When things got too crazy, she pulled out her most amazing magic trick: she would freeze everyone in place and buy herself a minute to breathe and plan.

She could… Control. Time. I was like, "I want to do that!"

As impressed as I was as a kid, preserving time got more important the older I got. Now I believe that controlling time might be the greatest superpower ever invented. What would you choose: invisibility, x-ray vision, the ability to fly? I would go with mastering time.

Oh my gosh, can you imagine if you had that power? What would you do if you could pause time? Get an extra hour of sleep? Go have a drink before dealing with baths and bedtimes? Have a private moment with your partner?

We could all be so much more productive if we woke up an hour earlier. And all of us could improve our time management. Those are good habits to build in the long term, but I have an idea that could net you some extra minutes today:

Pivot like a pro.

Imagine an athlete running full speed who suddenly changes direction to avoid a tackle or to run between two opponents. You can create time in your day by becoming a pro at changing directions.

So how can you pivot? I'm going to make it simple: Do whatever it takes to have your mind catch up with your body.

Is your head in the last play? The last meeting? Are you worried about tomorrow?

The first step is to become more aware of your time and what you are doing at the moment. Our phones are great ways to practice. I lose my focus looking at my phone and have to pull my attention back to the task at hand about a hundred times each day. Here's an embarrassing example:

My wife was waiting for me to get home to take the kids so she could leave for an appointment. I pulled up to the house and peeked at my phone. Of course, that's when that critical work email popped up that I was waiting for all day. I started reading it but then I remembered that my wife needed to leave. I rushed into the house, apologizing, when my daughter ran up like she hadn't seen me in months, "DADDY!!! hugg-iee!!!" and jumped into my arms. Could I call a time-out to finish reading my email? No, I don't want to be that guy.

So I play out that Hallmark moment, right? The rest of the world melts away while she puts her little hand in mine and leads me up to her room to play dolls. Cue the music, fade to black.

That's the way it should have gone.

Did I pivot, drop my phone, and do my job, be that superdad? No, I didn't. My head was still at work. I still had my phone in my hand when she jumped up and, the longer the hug went on, the more I was dying to finish the email, I am ashamed to admit.

I caught sight of myself in the mirror as I started to lift the phone over my daughter's shoulder. What the hell was I doing?

My phone steals minutes from my day all the time. And I don't mean just my phone. Texts, email, Facebook, Twitter. They all hurt my productivity at work. But being less attentive at work is a "victimless crime" when you compare it to the time it steals from your family.

The impact of active, or absent, fathers is undeniable. I see every day how much influence that dads like me have to make things right in our kids' lives.

When I look at my kids' friends, I see the huge difference in the risk factors. The dads who are present affect so many parts of their kids' lives: academic, emotional, spiritual, athletic. The dads who aren't around physically, or present emotionally, leave a giant hole in their kids' lives.

Also, a side note on multi-tasking. We all do it, or think we do it. It turns out that multi-tasking isn't a thing. You may be good at dividing your attention but multi-tasking is turning out to be a myth. When you divide your attention, you give less to each of the things that you are doing.

You actually deprive each of your tasks from the attention that they need to move forward. It's like the circus performer spinning plates on the tips of long sticks. She can run around and keep each plate from falling but none of them ever get the speed that they need.

Here's an idea* to learn to pivot. Sit down for 60 seconds with a blank piece of paper and put a mark down on the left side of the page for every thought you have about the past and one on the right side for every thought you have about the future. It's OK to have a lot of thoughts or not so many.

What's interesting about this game is noticing how much brain power we use in one minute to think about regrets from the past (left-hand side) or worries about the future (right side). You could be using that big brain of yours for so much more important work. So try this:

Gain a little more control over letting go of useless thoughts is a great way to pivot and be more present in the moment.

The coolest part about learning to pivot comes in when you are listening to your kids. If your head can catch up with your body, you can give them more of your focus and not let other things distract you. And when they recognize that you are actually listening to them, pivoting can be a game-changer.

For parents, it's a way to get better at ignoring the things that can distract you. Learning to pivot is like doing sit-ups or push-ups with your mind. With some practice, you can make your "attention muscle" stronger. I find that the more I practice, the more prepared I am when I have to pivot like a pro.

YOUR MISSION: GIVE 100% ATTENTION.

P.S. here are some ideas to get better at letting those useless thoughts go. Some people do a morning journal check-in. Some people learn to meditate. Check out a mindfulness class. Start with an app like HeadSpace, Buddhify, or Calm.

My life literally changed since I first wrote this book in 2015 when I finally found a type of meditation that works well for me. Shout out to Emily Fletcher at Ziva Meditation and her book, "Stress Less, Accomplish More" (2019).

Hat tip to Jenny Mills at Roots and Wing Mindfulness Center for teaching me this exercise.

9

BE THE GOOD WITCH

Watching The Wizard of Oz used to be a Thanksgiving ritual. It was only on TV once a year. And my favorite moment was how "Glinda the Good Witch" was so cool with Dorothy right after the house landed on her sister. She came down from the sky in her shimmering bubble and told Dorothy how special she was. Dorothy didn't know that she had all of this potential.

We all have inner critics reminding us how lame or flawed we are. You know it's not all true. But where do you find the voice to argue with the negative soundtrack that plays in your head 24 hours a day?

When you were young, who gave you shelter from criticism and made you feel whole again? Did a teacher see your potential? Did an aunt or uncle remind you how special you are? Where do normal kids get to hear that Good Witch voice?

I don't have to tell you that, as a parent, you have enormous power. You own the most influential voice in your child's life. Why shouldn't you be the Good Witch?

Think about the times when you have to tell your kids what to do, hold them accountable, and remind them of their responsibilities. It is your job, I'm not arguing with that. After all, who else is going to do it?

There are also times when we let our own frustration and anger hijack the tone and way we talk to our kids. In the most extreme, we can go overboard telling them that they are disappointing us. One of the most depressing things I hear kids say is that their home life is more stressful than school, filled with pressures, over protection, and questioning from parents.

Your home should be the place for your kids to:

- learn empathy and compassion
- gain self-control
- develop their own work ethic, the ability to persevere
- learn how to deal with frustration
- find their own character strengths

When do you need to be stern and when could you be a positive, encouraging voice? Think about the times when you don't need to add a critical voice to the negative soundtrack in their heads.

Try it out. If the moment is right, be their cheerleader, their Glinda the Good Witch. If it works, find more times when you can pull out your pom poms. Give me a G! Give me an O!

If you aren't the touchy, feely type, if you don't see yourself as a cheerleader, climb the chair and be your child's emotional lifeguard.

Protect their feelings. Give your sons and daughters and non-binary kids a safe space where they can decompress and be themselves. Kids need that space but sometimes they don't know where to find it. Long term, you want them to have a space where they come with their problems. Make your home that space.

YOUR MISSION: GIVE YOUR KIDS REFUGE.

P.S. If Dorothy's house landed on the Wicked Witch in 2020, the first thing Glinda would do after stepping out of her glimmering bubble is to gently take the school-issued Chromebook out of Dorothy's hands. Then she would kindly ask Dorothy to take Toto outside before he peed the Yellow Brick Road.

Managing your kids' education in 2020 presents the Grand Champion challenge of all challenges for you to "Be the Good Witch."

School used to give parents a lot: the time they needed to make money, to share the responsibility to educate their children, and to get a little break. Not only is all of that gone but you have been promoted to unpaid, full-time teacher, tutor, counselor, and principal. By now, you have probably tried to quit more than once. But guess what? You woke up re-hired.

You see, this is the "Hotel California" of schooling: "you can check out anytime you like, but you can never leave!"

Distance learning is a bad bargain for both parents and kids. It's stripped down of all the parts that help kids get through the school day: the structure of the school day, the teachers they like, movement between classes, and most of all, the social interaction.

Now it's all on you to create that structure.

Your kids need you. The school needs you. And you? Well, your needs have been written off in this new online way to do school.

That's the problem … and the solution: you can't give your kids the cover they need from school's demands until you stand up for yourself. You can show them how to create boundaries for themselves. The first step is to place yourself at the center of your own family's self-care strategy.

You may be struggling with self-care right now. That's why this is a two-fer.

Show them that you can control when to turn the screens off and how to budget your time. Touch nature every day. Take control over your morning and bedtime routines. Get yourself on track and then you can confidently assure your kids, "It's going to be OK. We totally have this under control."

Dr. Robert Zeitlin

10

CLIMB OUT ON A LIMB

Remember earlier when I said that, one day, your kids may save the world? I mentioned Malala Yousafzai as an example. You may not recognize her name but you probably know her story. Malala is a Pakistani girl who began speaking out publicly when she was 11 years old about the need for girls to be educated in her country. She made so many waves that the Taliban attempted to assassinate her at 14. She survived, continued speaking out, and was granted the Nobel Peace Prize at the age of 17.

It's hard to imagine what strengths drive a young woman like Malala. Rather than understanding her motivation, I want you to imagine if you were her parent. If you knew, somehow, that your child is destined to play a critical part in changing the future of the world, what would you do?

When a family recognizes that they have a kid who is the next Roger Federer or first round draft pick, they sacrifice everything to maximize that future possibility, dedicating their finances and time, moving across the country to be closer to coaches and colleges, doing whatever it takes to foster their careers.

What if your kid is destined to be Malala instead of LeBron? What would you sacrifice? Sure, you can try to shake off the possibility that you are raising the next kick-ass kid that the world needs.

But what if I'm right?

In the face of all of that responsibility, I told you not to panic. It's not about draining your bank account or quitting your job. Remember how

I said that you have special abilities?

You don't just have special abilities. It's more than that.

When I was 3 or 4, I thought my dad, who was a pretty big guy, was larger than life. I saw football players like Mean Joe Green on TV and was sure that he was one of them. Most kids look at their parent and see a superhero.

Is that really just silly kid stuff? Your kids believe that you can do anything. I know it sounds like comic book fiction but what if your kids aren't deluded? What if they see your real potential?

So, coming back to those special abilities that you have. Well, there is a lot more potential in you than you may realize. I don't want to scare you when I tell you that you actually are a superhero. You have superpowers. And the world needs you to save the day. We believe in you.

Your mission is to raise the kick-ass kids that the world will need. This news might be a little disorienting. You might be laughing it off. Think about the "origin" story for any superhero: before you know that you are a superhero, you feel confused and scared. You know that you can "do things" but you look for a logical explanation to get your head around your "special abilities." Eventually your logical sense just runs out of runway gives you no other choice but to take flight. You accept what they are: you have superpowers.

Here's my "origin" story: I have always been pretty shy about taking risks. I usually obey the voice in my head that says, "be careful" and asks, "are you sure you want to do that?" We all get these messages. They come straight from the most ancient part of our brain. In "Linchpin" (2010), Seth Godin explains how your Lizard Brain can shut down your motivation if it feels threatened with too much change or risk.

Because it has so much control – it was formed earlier in human evolution than the fun, creative part – the Lizard Brain is very hard to outsmart or overpower.

But taking risks in the 21st century (buying a house, writing a book, changing careers) is less dangerous than escaping a sabre-tooth tiger or hunting for a mammoth. Sometimes, taking risks is exactly what you should be doing.

Even if you're on the right track,
you'll get run over if you just sit there.

– Will Rogers

Even though it's 2020, your Lizard Brain is still following ancient orders. It hasn't evolved and kept up with the times. It still wants us to avoid change, listen to our fear, think about it some more, and wait. In fact, it takes advantage of moments like this pandemic presents, stoking fears in an effort to keep us safe.

Picture yourself on a train, pre-social distancing, seated next to a stranger who is reading your favorite book. Even though she's a stranger, it would be easy to say something like, "I loved that book."

Before you can even formulate what to say, your Lizard Brain is working to shut you down, pulling on all your familiar fears, reminding you that "it's too risky to talk to strangers," and "she could be crazy." It starts to make sense to you, why you wouldn't approach a stranger.

On the other hand, what if this person holds a key to your life that you can't yet see? She may inspire an idea that changes your career, connect you with a valuable advisor, or share an insight that improves your health. If you knew that in advance, would you extend yourself to start a conversation?

What if she needs something that only you can provide? Choosing to take the risk could have huge benefits. Your actions could have a ripple effect in your life and hers, and the lives you both touch.

Here's where my superpower came in: I learned how to deal with my Lizard Brain. I've learned not to battle. Respecting its power to shut me down with fear, I find some positive messages to throw into the mix: "maybe she knows someone that can help me," "she looks friendly," or "what's the worst that could happen, really?" Those ideas reduce the fear, taking the venom out of the Lizard Brain's sting. Then it's about making a decision, taking a leap.

"You've got to go out on a limb sometimes because that's where the fruit is" (from Will Rogers, again). Climbing out on a limb is my superpower.

For most of my life, my negative soundtrack ran a one-sided campaign in my head. Each time I climb out on that limb, though, I strengthen my defenses against my Lizard Brain by adding internal messages with credible alternatives. Now my negative thoughts are no longer winning by default.

Since I started using my superpower, I have been more willing to take smart chances. Taking calculated risks like talking to strangers or raising my hand to ask "one more" question have made things happen for me in the last few years.

Exercising this superpower has also allowed me to uncover more superpowers: I am eager to find new things to learn, I love living with zest and enthusiasm, I think analytically, and I possess the courage to persevere over the long term. Using these superpowers, I am proud to say that:

- my wife and I motivate each other to challenge our fears and conquer the big goals that scare us
- I sing in the car more
- I stopped working on a few seriously flawed personal and business relationships
- I am making new friends for the first time in about a decade
- I ask random people in the store or schools how they are (and they respond with open hearts)
- I stopped beating myself up over procrastinating and accepted that my energy can ebb and flow, and that my motivation will return soon
- family and friends ask how I am doing all the stuff that I'm doing

The more that I use these superpowers, the more I laugh and the less I yell. I play more. I savor moments more. I am more present with my wife and kids. And I decided to write a book, publish an updated version, and give a TEDx talk. I was invited to India by a stranger because an article I wrote with my child travelled around the world. I create new surprising and wonderful results every week.

YOUR MISSION:
FIND YOUR SUPERPOWER.

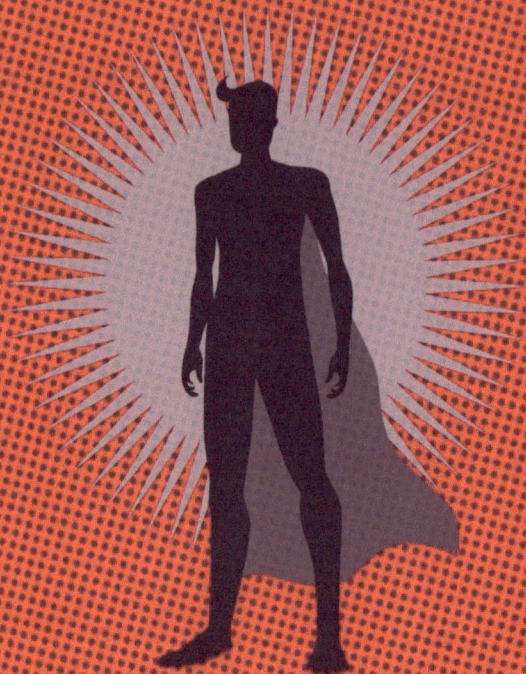

11

PUT ON YOUR CAPE

How can you figure out your superpowers?

You can begin doing more laughing than yelling, more playing than working, and choosing to be Glinda more often than a critic. Taking any of these ideas seriously and incorporating them in your life every day will begin to change the ratio of positive over negative experiences in your life.

Positive Psychology researcher Barbara Fredrickson revealed the upward spiral you can achieve in your life if you have three positive emotions and experiences in your day for every negative one. Even if you can't change how much negative stuff happens in your life, impressive things start happening when you reach the tipping point of 3:1. So it doesn't matter if you have 100 bad things happen in your day, as long as you have 300 good ones.

At 1:1, most people are depressed. At 2:1, you feel better. At 3:1, you start to thrive.

Here is another simple recipe to increase your ratio:

Do your best thing more.

It's that simple. Take the time to figure out what you are especially good at.

Then do it more.
You could also take this survey* to reveal your signature strengths.

If you are hesitant, don't worry. This survey is all about your positives, not any negatives.

You should know, I never talk about my test results. I am totally private. I don't talk about my cholesterol level or share my credit score. Call me paranoid. I don't want to give anyone information that can be used against me.

But I have absolutely no hesitation about sharing my character strengths with you. There's nothing in these results that I need to keep private and I'm proud of the upward spiral I have experienced in my life since I started focusing my attention on these strengths and finding new ways to exercise them.

Let's imagine you know your strengths and want to find ways to exercise them. If you are someone who uses humor, you could find more ways to find funny things or get people laughing. If you are a leader, you could get involved in a nonprofit organization. If you love learning, you could make a routine to learn about new things every day. If you are brave, you could find little ways to be brave every day. You don't need to rush into burning buildings, just stand up for someone or tell the bus driver to wait.

It's pretty simple logic. Your superpowers are the untapped parts of yourself that you use randomly, sometimes at work, sometimes at home. You probably get a little jolt when you express your creativity, explore your spirituality, or find ways to let your curiosity out of its cage. Put in the effort to embrace your powers and find ways to use them. When you make a routine of it, you can increase your positivity ratio, expand your life, and thrive.

YOUR MISSION:
CREATE AN UPWARD SPIRAL
IN YOUR LIFE.

* If you want to take the survey, it's free and there's an optional report that gives you more information and ideas on how to exercise your top strengths. If that link didn't work, copy and paste this URL: https://www.viacharacter.org/pro/drrobertzeitlin/account/register.
I make no money from the survey or the add-on reports. They are both offered by the VIA Institute, the group that conducted the original research to identify the 24 character strengths found most frequently in the Bible, the Koran, the writings of St. Thomas Aquinas, Confucius, Aristotle and all the great religious and philosophical texts. Details can be found at https://viacharacter.org/.

12

WHAT'S NEXT?

I was in your shoes. I was a parent looking for answers. This book shares the steps I took to find my superpowers. Now I want to make it easy, fun, and inviting for you to take steps toward becoming the parent that your kids need. I want to inspire you.

Your journey is individual to you. As I said at the start, this isn't a recipe to relieve your fear. There is no single "answer" that I can give you to do next.

There is one hard, cold fact that I can tell you if you want to raise kick-ass kids who take calculated risks: you need to "be the branch" to support them. It is more powerful to lead by example, to "show" rather than "tell."

Show them that it's safe by climbing out on your own limb to develop your own superpowers.

You have amazing kids. I know. I've seen them in action. They have creative, inspiring ideas. Your kids' imaginations are the adult think-tanks of the future. Ask them what superpower they would want. You might be surprised by the answer.

If I were you, this what I would do next: Discover and develop your superpowers. That will help you construct a family where your kids will find their passion.

Step One:

Ask yourself: Is your family a safe place to try new things? Can you look foolish in front of each other? Do you know what excites your partner or your kids? Work toward making your household a place where you ask yourself these questions all the time.

Try out the moves in this book to create a family that laughs more and plays together: be the parent, become a stronger team with your partner, be the good witch, learn to pivot. Start by taking care of yourself, remembering to apply your own oxygen mask first. That way your kids will feel safe to take risks and dream big. Remember, one of their ideas just might save the world one day.

Step Two:

Model your superpowers to provide the branch that supports your kids' growth. Set up a family culture that naturally encourages your kids to go out on a limb, to take risks, to fail, and to pick themselves up again. Learning from their mistakes – and having the courage to make mistakes – is how they will kick some ass.

Step Three:

Share your stories with me at **@drrobertzeitlin** on Twitter or Instagram.

ACKNOWLEDGEMENTS

First and foremost, I want to thank my "unforgettable" wife Betsy for her belief in me, that I can achieve my goals. Secondly, I appreciate the strong examples that my parents provided to me growing up and the support of both of our families in raising our own incredible children. I want to recognize the contribution of Kristin Kane Ford, who wore so many hats in the production of this work that I don't have room to list, spanning from the birthing of core ideas, editing, and the layout of the book you are holding right now. In addition, Shannon Myers was instrumental in getting this whole train started down the right track.

I appreciate the contributions of the professionals with whom I have supported parents in my community including Nicole Merritt, Erika Schell-Rompré, Kiki McKendrick, Martie Gillin, Martie Bernicker, Ann Bernicker, Collen Philbin, Kim Bullock, Rabbi Geri Newburge, Rabbi David Straus, and Ross M. Levy. My altMBA family also helped me ride out more than a few bumps in the road, including Margo Aaron, Jake Kahana, Charles Grove, Maria Xenidou, David Dvorkin, Ido Kanyon, Taylor Harrington, and Jocelyn Ring.

Finally, I want to acknowledge the outstanding contributions of the educators and clinicians with whom I am proud to have fought beside on behalf of the schoolchildren in Philadelphia and beyond including Paul Fink (of blessed memory), Lorene Cary, Jody Greenblatt, Tracy-Marie Moody, Shari Ingram, Sarah Lorraine, Katie Carpenter, Christina Minecci, Michael Reichert, and Belinda Miller (of blessed memory).

REFERENCES

Ferriss, Timothy. (2009). The 4-Hour Workweek. New York: Crown Publishing.

Fletcher, Emily. (2019). Stress less, accomplish more: Meditation for extraordinary performance. New York: William Morrow.

Fredrickson, Barbara. (2009). Positivity. New York: Three Rivers Press.

Godin, Seth. (2010). Linchpin. New York: Penguin.

Kimmel, Michael. (2008). Guyland. New York: HarperCollins.

Levs, Josh. (2015). All in. New York: HarperOne.

Seligman, Martin. (2002). Authentic happiness. New York: Atria.

ABOUT THE AUTHOR

Dr. Robert Zeitlin has dedicated the last 25 years to raising his kids, helping the children under his care, and working with parents to raise the children that the future needs. With his wife Betsy, Robert has raised two amazing ~~teens~~ adults who are kicking ass and taking names. Working in schools, nonprofits, and his practice, Robert has maximized his background in Clinical Psychology and his knowledge of Positive Psychology to create family and school cultures that produce courageous leaders and communicators.

www.ingramcontent.com/pod-product-compliance
Lightning Source LLC
Chambersburg PA
CBHW041623110426

42740CB00042BA/33